Dedicated to all the preachers who have stayed faithful to God and the ministry even after a divorce. Also, to all the "non-divorced" preachers who have stood by those divorced preachers and supported them in their trial!

Chapter 1
DIVORCE IS A SIN

Divorce is simply a fact of life. We all have, in someway, been touched by divorce. Whether it be growing up in a broken home or having been through one yourself or having someone you know and love go through one, we have all been affected by this awful circumstance. In writing this book I will undoubtedly receive the typical criticisms of "justifying sin" and "covering for fornicators and adulterers". They will accuse me of saying that "anytime you get tired of your wife just simply divorce her and find another". But the reason they say these things is NOT because I actually believe them but because they must find a way to discredit what I'm about to set forth in this book because they CANNOT refute any of it! I always have and always will maintain the position of reconciliation and forgiveness as the best paths when it comes to marriage problems. I truly believe that the Lord is grieved by the complete disregard for the home in our society today. When we look at what the Bible says we find out how the Lord Himself feels about divorce in Malachi 2:16,

"For the LORD, the God of Israel, saith that he hateth putting away: for one covereth violence with his garment, saith the LORD of hosts: therefore take heed to your spirit, that ye deal not treacherously."

The verse could not be any plainer. God hates "putting away" or, that is to say, divorce. But this does not mean that He forbids divorce. Actually quite the opposite is true when you consider Ezra 10. The children of Israel had taken "strange wives" and in order to get right with God they make a covenant to "put away all the wives" of the heathen people they had taken (Ezra 10:3). Divorce in Ezra 10 wasn't just permitted but it was EXPECTED! When we look at the context of Malachi 2:16 we see that they were putting away the "wives of their youth" (Malachi 2:14-15) and had taken "daughters of a strange god" (Malachi 2:11). All divorce is the direct result of sin. God instituted the home in Genesis 2 when he made Eve from the rib of Adam and gave her to him for a spouse. Jesus confirms this fact in Matthew 19 when he is dealing with questions from the Pharisees concerning the subject of divorce. We will delve further into this conversation later but I want to point something out for the sake of this chapter. Notice Matthew 19:6 says,

Wherefore they (Adam & Eve) *are no more twain, but one flesh. What therefore God hath joined together, let <u>not</u> man put asunder.*

Jesus CLEARLY says that once a man and woman are married they shouldn't get divorced. The Pharisees, knowing the scriptures better than most Baptists today, immediately point to the Old Testament Mosaic law where God DID permit them to divorce and asks why then it was given if God's plan was to stay married forever. Jesus' response gives us a clear reason why the "writing of divorcement" was given by God....

He saith unto them, Moses because of the HARDNESS OF YOUR HEARTS suffered you to put away your wives: but from the beginning it was not so. (Matthew 19:8)

Notice the reason that God gave for divorce was the hardening of hearts which happens through SIN! Don't miss the cross reference in Hebrews 3:13,

But exhort one another daily while it is called To day; lest any of you be HARDENED through the deceitfulness of SIN.

No true Bible Believer today thinks that divorce is a good thing. Divorce is a terrible thing that has been treated way too lightly by our modern day society. Divorce is not usually the result of sin but is ALWAYS the result of sin. But God knew that sin would enter into people's hearts so He GRACIOUSLY allowed certain ways out of a bad marriage situation. The modern day Pharisees would rather see you be married to a serial adulterer or be celibate for the rest of your life after a divorce than to commit the "abominable act" of getting remarried and having "two living wives", which is the most unbiblical statement in the world unless you're talking about true blue POLYGAMY!

But having said all this we must not forget that even though divorce is a direct result of sin it does NOT necessarily mean that both parties were in sin. Not every marriage ends because both parties are wrong. When it comes to divorce there can be an INNOCENT PARTY!

Chapter 2
THE INNOCENT PARTY

One of the most ignorant statements made in the conversation about divorce and remarriage is that there can be no innocent party when it comes to divorce. The modern day pharisees will always lay blame on both spouses regardless of the circumstances. Our society as a whole, including our churches, will usually lay most of the blame on the man! I'll give the prime example. If a man leaves his wife for another woman then people will say he's a no good, low down scoundrel who should be taken out behind the wood shed. But then on the other hand if the woman leaves the man it was probably because he didn't help with the house work, the kids and probably wasn't showing her enough attention. See how that thing works? Our society UNJUSTLY lays more blame on the man in the matter of divorce. Why couldn't the woman be a dirty, rotten scoundrel who in a fit of lust left her husband for another man? And let me say this, regardless of how bad the marriage was, it is NEVER bad enough to justify, in any way, one of the spouses cheating. I will deal with this more in a later chapter but it needs mentioning in this chapter as well because we are dealing with the "Innocent Party".

Now before you automatically put this whole chapter off because you do not believe there is an innocent party in divorce, lets examine what the Scriptures have to say about it. If you're anything like me then you usually just skim the scripture references in a book but PLEASE read very carefully the following passage from Numbers 5:11-31 where we find a biblical example of there being an "innocent party", it's probably more Bible than some of you have read this week anyway!

11 And the Lord spake unto Moses, saying,

12Speak unto the children of Israel, and say unto them, If any man's wife go aside, and commit a trespass against him,

13And a man lie with her carnally, and it be hid from the eyes of her husband, and be kept close, and she be defiled, and there be no witness against her, neither she be taken with the manner;

14And the spirit of jealousy come upon him, and he be jealous of his wife, and she be defiled: or if the spirit of jealousy come upon him, and he be jealous of his wife, and she be not defiled:

15Then shall the man bring his wife unto the priest, and he shall bring her offering for her, the tenth part of an ephah of barley meal; he shall pour no oil upon it, nor put frankincense thereon; for it is an offering of jealousy, an offering of memorial, bringing iniquity to remembrance.

16And the priest shall bring her near, and set her before the Lord:

17And the priest shall take holy water in an earthen vessel; and of the dust that is in the floor of the tabernacle the priest shall take, and put it into the water:

18And the priest shall set the woman before the Lord, and uncover the woman's head, and put the offering of memorial in her hands, which is the jealousy offering: and the priest shall have in his hand the bitter water that causeth the curse:

19And the priest shall charge her by an oath, and say unto the woman, If no man have lain with thee, and if thou hast not gone aside to uncleanness with another instead of thy husband, be thou free from this bitter water that causeth the curse:

20But if thou hast gone aside to another instead of thy husband, and if thou be defiled, and some man have lain with thee beside thine husband:

21Then the priest shall charge the woman with an oath of cursing, and the priest shall say unto the woman, The Lord make thee a curse and an oath among thy people, when the Lord doth make thy thigh to rot, and thy belly to swell;

22And this water that causeth the curse shall go into thy bowels, to make thy belly to swell, and thy thigh to rot: And the woman shall say, Amen, amen.

23And the priest shall write these curses in a book, and he shall blot them out with the bitter water:

24And he shall cause the woman to drink the bitter water that causeth the curse: and the water that causeth *the curse shall enter into her, and become bitter.*

25Then the priest shall take the jealousy offering out of the woman's hand, and shall wave the offering before the Lord, and offer it upon the altar:

26And the priest shall take an handful of the offering, even the memorial thereof, and burn it upon the altar, and afterward shall cause the woman to drink the water.

27And when he hath made her to drink the water, then it shall come to pass, that, if she be defiled, and have done trespass against her husband, that the water that causeth the curse shall enter into her, and become bitter, and her belly shall swell, and her thigh shall rot: and the woman shall be a curse among her people.

28And if the woman be not defiled, but be clean; then she shall be free, and shall conceive seed.

29This is the law of jealousies, when a wife goeth aside to another instead of her husband, and is defiled;

30Or when the spirit of jealousy cometh upon him, and he be jealous over his wife, and shall set the woman before the Lord, and the priest shall execute upon her all this law.

31<u>Then shall the man be guiltless from iniquity, and this woman shall bear her iniquity.</u>

In case you didn't quite catch it, we find the explanation of the "law of jealousies". If a man suspected his wife of "stepping out" (southern for "cheating") then he would take his wife down to the tabernacle where the priest would make a concoction using the dust from the floor and make her swear her innocence and then drink the "dusty cocktail". If the woman was found to be innocent then nothing would happen and she would conceive seed and be free. But if she was guilty then the Bible said her stomach would swell and her thighs would rot. But notice the most pertinent verse to this chapter, verse 31. It clearly says that if the woman was found guilty then the man is "guiltless" and the woman "shall bear her iniquity". This doesn't sound like God is blaming both parties. In fact it is the exact opposite, the blame only lies with ONE!

Regardless of what anyone thinks there are times when people simply allow sin in their heart and they commit sin that dissolves the marriage. The spouse could be totally dedicated to the Lord and doing everything in their best ability to be the right kind of spouse and yet the other party will STILL decide to leave or to cheat. I cannot tell you how many times I've heard the self-righteous "once married" crowd vehemently say that if the marriage falls apart then both parties were guilty. Although, like I said, they are much more gracious if the woman leaves than when the man does! But before you think that a man could NEVER lose his marriage if he was being the right kind of husband let us examine the DIVORCED GOD!

Chapter 3

THE DIVORCED GOD

I think that everyone reading this book would agree that God is sinless. If He was a husband (and He was) then He would be the "perfect spouse". He would provide every need to His wife and even some of her wants. He would give protection from danger. He would give an unmatched love for His bride. His bride would never have any accusation to bring against Him. We find that everything I just listed IS true of God because He was married to Israel in the Old Testament. Yet God's marriage ended in divorce. The following passages confirm this truth,

Thus saith the LORD, Where is the bill of your mother's divorcement, whom I have put away? Or which of my creditors is it to whom I have sold you? Behold, for your iniquities have ye sold yourselves, and for your transgressions is your mother put away. (Isaiah 50:1)

And I saw, when for all the causes whereby backsliding Israel committed adultery I had put her away, and given her a bill of divorce; yet her treacherous sister Judah feared not, but went and played the harlot also.

(Jeremiah 3:8)

The problem with the marriage was not with God but with Israel. Israel, even though she had the perfect husband, decided to leave and commit adultery. Two verses lay it out as plain as the nose on your face that God Himself is indeed divorced. He marries Israel but then through sexual sin she breaks the marriage covenant and God gives her a bill of divorcement. For all you self-righteous Pharisees who so arrogantly say, "I would never sit under a divorced pastor!" I ask this question, would you sit under a divorced God? Is God now disqualified to pastor your local Baptist Church? Some of you would expect a pastor to step down immediately if his wife left him and if he didn't you'd vote him out in a split second! Well guess what? God got divorced, through no fault of His own (obviously), and He didn't even think twice about stepping down or being "disqualified"! Funny business trying to twist the Scriptures, isn't it? Whenever someone says the think a man is disqualified from any office in the church simply because he's been divorced they are promoting their own ideas and traditions above the scriptures and above God Himself.

This whole scenario is perfectly illustrated by the story of Hosea. Hosea is told to take a harlot for a wife to picture the fact that Israel, married to God, was a whore as well (Hosea 1:2). Her name is Gomer and she bears Hosea three children. She then goes back to her "old job" and leaves Hosea and the kids. Now when Hosea sends his children to plead with their mother to return he makes one of the most important statements in all the Bible about divorce. He says in Hosea 2:2,

Plead with your mother, plead: <u>for she is not my wife,</u>
<u>*neither am I her husband*</u>*: let her therefore put away her*
whoredoms out of her sight, and her adulteries from
between her breasts;

This completely destroys the whole "two living wives" jargon and shows that a legitimate divorce not only ends a marriage in the sight of the law but also in the sight of God. Once Hosea got divorced it was said that he and Gomer were no longer husband and wife. Almost sounds like "Til death do us part" may have an exception. And indeed it does! In fact it has 2 and we will use the next three chapters to deal with THE EXCEPTIONS!

Chapter 4

THE FIRST EXCEPTION: FORNICATION

In Matthew 19 we find the conversation that takes place between the Pharisees and Jesus concerning divorce. As we already pointed out, Jesus tells them that God's original plan was for a man and a woman to stay together forever but because of the hardness of their hearts He permitted them to have divorce. It's within this very story that we find our first exception to 'til death do us part, fornication. In Matthew 19:9 the Lord makes this statement,

And I say unto you, Whosoever shall put away his wife, <u>except it be for fornication</u>, and shall marry another, committeth adultery: and whoso marrieth her which is put away doth commit adultery.

Now here is where we must define our terms carefully and biblically! Jesus did NOT say that "adultery" was the exception but "fornication" was. Many have looked at this verse and negated this God given exception by saying that these people weren't really married because it says "fornication" which is sex before marriage. They have developed some strange extra-biblical view about Jewish engagements and ceremonial traditions called "The Espousal Theory". This whole subject has a chapter all to itself where we will deal with the logical fallacy and downright rejection of scripture that is necessary to believe such a convoluted mess.

The simple truth is this, "fornication" doesn't simply mean sex before marriage and "adultery" doesn't simply mean immoral sex after marriage. What we must do is look at how the Bible defines these terms.

Firstly, look at fornication. Fornication is defined for us in I Corinthians 6:18,

> *Flee fornication. Every sin that a man doeth is <u>without the body</u>; but he that committeth fornication sinneth against <u>his own body</u>.*

Fornication is any sexual sin committed with the body, regardless of marital status. Notice the people in Matthew 19:9 were said to be man and wife, married! Jesus had previously made the same statement in Matthew 5:31-32 when dealing with the Old Testament law whilst preaching the Sermon on the Mount. He says in those verses,

> *It hath been said, Whosoever shall put away his wife, let him give her a writing of divorcement: But I say unto you, That whosoever shall put away his wife, <u>saving for the cause of fornication</u>, causeth her to commit adultery: and whosoever shall marry her that is divorced committeth adultery.*

In the Old Testament you could put away your wife for basically "any uncleanness" (Deut. 24:1). And before you go and say that "uncleanness" is some sexual sin just do a simple word search on your Bible app of "unclean/uncleanness" to find out the extent of what could deem her "unclean". It's a WHOLE lot more than just sexual impurity. That is why the Pharisees asked Jesus if it was lawful to put away your wife for "every cause" (Matthew 19:3). Jesus, just as he did many times in the Sermon on the Mount, takes the Old Testament law a step further and "tightens the rules", if you will. In the Old Testament you could put her away for "uncleanness" but NOW it's only fornication. Hopefully by now you have seen that fornication can be used in the context of married people NOT simply single people.

Now secondly, look at adultery. Adultery is commonly defined as "immoral sex after marriage" or basically "cheating on your spouse". But we find that this definition simply does not hold true when compared with scripture either. Let's go back to the Sermon on the Mount and take a look at what Jesus said concerning adultery. Matthew 5:27-28 reads,

Ye have heard that it was said by them of old time, Thou shalt not commit adultery: But I say unto you, That whosoever looketh on a woman to lust after her hath committed adultery with her already in his heart.

Now don't miss this! This means that adultery can be committed by a single person without ever laying a HAND on the other person! It can be committed with the eyes and take place in the heart without the other person ever knowing. That is why the exception to marriage is NOT "adultery" but "fornication". If adultery was the exception then every woman on planet earth would have a reason to leave her husband. Every stray glance at someone with lust in the heart would give the spouse reason to divorce. But this is not the exception, "fornication" is. There must be an actual, physical, bodily act in order for there to be "fornication". It is committed "with the body". Adultery can be committed with the body when pertaining to sex outside the marriage bed but it doesn't have to be exclusively that.

To further back up the biblical fact that fornication gives a man or woman the right to divorce and remarry look at what Job says in Job 31:9-10,

> *If mine heart have been <u>deceived by a woman</u>, or if I have laid wait at my neighbors door; Then <u>let my wife grind unto another</u>, and <u>let others bow down upon her.</u>*

Job makes it clear that if he's cheated on his wife that she can go be another man's wife and there's nothing he can do about it. Its obvious that a sexual act committed by a spouse leaves the innocent spouse with the option of divorce where remarriage is completely fine.
But in the midst of dealing with this subject of infidelity we must also be reminded of GRACE! Can a person biblically and justifiably divorce their spouse when their spouse has committed fornication? Yes. Do they have to though? No. There is no doubt that the grace of God can take a stained marriage and restore it and reconcile the

spouses. When fornication is committed the innocent party is not commanded to stay with the guilty party BUT they are not commanded to automatically divorce them either. But what it does require, regardless if the marriage is saved or not is FORGIVENESS! It may be hard and it may require a lot of "working through" but homes do not have to be destroyed by fornication even though it may have happened. Especially in the case of having children still living at home, they need both parents under the same roof. I'm glad Jesus Christ doesn't automatically divorce us when we sin against him! We have been shown much grace in our marriage to Christ. This clause doesn't exclude grace but it also doesn't demand it either. Simply put, if you are the innocent party in a marriage tainted by fornication and the guilty party is seeking reconciliation then the choice is with you. You have the biblical right to divorce or stay together. Pray and seek God's face, consider the situation and do what you feel is right for you, your children and your home. This may give the brethren a coronary but I do believe there are situations where divorce is actually the right option. In cases of multiple offenses I would absolutely say divorce needs to be strongly considered. In cases where the spouse or the children are being physically abused by the other spouse I would most assuredly tell them to leave. No two situations are exactly the same so it is hard to make blanket statements on when you should leave and when you shouldn't. All I can say is what the scriptures have said, if your spouse has committed fornication then you have the biblical right to leave.

Chapter 5
THE SECOND EXCEPTION: ABANDONMENT

We find in I Corinthians 7 our next exception to the marriage vow, abandonment. A close examination of I Corinthians 7 is necessary to understand the exact requirements of the desertion in order for it to be deemed a biblically justified divorce. There is a command for saved couples not to split up in I Corinthians 7:10-11, we will deal with these verses in just a moment. Then right after that we find the Pauline exception laid out very clearly in verses 12-15,

But to the rest speak I, not the Lord: If any brother hath a wife that believeth not, and she be pleased to dwell with him, let him not put her away. And the woman which hath an husband that believeth not, and he be pleased to dwell with her, let her not leave him. For the unbelieving husband is sanctified by the wife, and the unbelieving wife is sanctified by the husband: else were your children unclean; but now are they holy. But if the unbelieving depart, let him depart. A brother or a sister is not under bondage in such cases: but God hath called us to peace.

Now here is where I will depart from even some of those that hold to divorce and remarriage. I believe the "abandonment clause" is speaking directly of a situation where a lost person leaves a saved person. The context of these verses is not an "unbeliever of the ministry" or a "backslidden Christian that doesn't want to serve Jesus anymore". No, it is quite obvious that the context is a marriage between a saved person and a lost person. The scripture is very clear that if you are a saved person married to a lost person and they are "pleased to dwell" with you then you are NOT suppose to divorce that person. Them being lost does not give you the right to leave them. It should also be said that a saved person shouldn't do anything to try and cause the lost person to leave. Verse 16 tells us that we may save the unbelieving spouse by our testimony. This would NOT be the case if you were a "jerk for Jesus" and drove them off so you could claim "abandonment"! If they are pleased to dwell with you (not if they come to church or if they have high moral standards) then you are to do everything you can to make the marriage work and try and win them to Christ. It is only when THEY decide to leave are you free to remarry. The Bible says, "Let them depart. A brother or a sister is NOT under bondage in such cases..." In other words, you are free from that marriage and may remarry if you choose.

What now will naturally be brought up at this point is the question, "What about saved people leaving saved people?" Paul deals with this in I Corinthians 7:10-11,

And unto the married I command, yet not I, but the Lord, <u>Let not the wife depart from her husband</u>; But and <u>if she depart, let her remain unmarried, or be reconciled</u> to her husband: and <u>let not the husband put away his wife</u>.

We see that saved people aren't suppose to get divorces. It is a terrible testimony to the lost world and a horrible example to our children when two saved adults can't work out their marriage because of "irreconcilable differences". But the scripture does, however, give commandment for if this does happen. The person who decides to leave must remain unmarried. Does this then allow the deserted party to remarry? The Bible simply never says. And before you try and quote verse 15 remember that is dealing with a "mixed union" and clearly says the lost person must depart. This verse here is speaking of saved people where neither one of them should depart (except where the allowance is given on fornication). What we have to keep in mind though is that 9 times out of 10 when someone is abandoning a spouse it is usually for another person! Very rarely do you find people just packing up and leaving because they simply are tired of the spouse. They usually have their eyes on another person. In the case of the saved spouse who departed I can absolutely say that they are to remain unmarried but in the case of the deserted saved spouse I cannot be authoritative. Where the scriptures are silent, I'm silent. Sure I have my opinions, but they are just that, opinions. It is certain that once the departed spouse decides to "hook up" with someone rather than be reconciled then the deserted spouse is 100% free to remarry. II Samuel 20:3 tell us that King David had 10 concubines, who were considered wives (cross reference Genesis 25:1 with I Chron. 1:32), that, although he gave them alimony, he deserted. The Bible says that they lived out the rest of their days in "widowhood". They were treated as if their husband had died, but he hadn't. He had simply deserted them. If you have been deserted by a saved spouse for a reason other than fornication on your part then I cannot tell you that you have the right to remarry biblically. But I also cannot tell you that you do NOT have the right to remarry biblically. To this situation I simply say, "I don't know". Amazing how many made-made traditions a King James Bible will mess up!

Chapter 6
REMARRIAGE AFTER A DIVORCE

Look at I Corinthians 7:27-28,

Art thou bound unto a wife? Seek not to be loosed. Art thou loosed from a wife? Seek not a wife. But and if thou marry, <u>thou hast not sinned</u>...

The Pauline command here is that if a man is married he is not suppose to seek to get out of the marriage. He is to remain faithful to his vows. If he, for whatever reason, is no longer married then he is to remain single, following the example of the Apostle Paul (I Cor. 7:7-8,32-40). But notice very carefully the phrase at the beginning of verse 28, "But and if thou marry, THOU HAST NOT SINNED..." To tell a man that has been legally loosed from a marriage that remarrying is a sin is not just dumb it's anti-Bible! But this does not always mean that remarriage is permitted after a divorce. God does place some limitations on the remarriage in certain cases.

Firstly, as we just saw in the previous chapter, remarriage is not permitted in the case of saved persons who willingly abandoned their spouse for no biblical reason. It doesn't matter how much you may not have liked the person, unless they cheated on you or completely deserted you for another you are not allowed to get remarried after you divorce. (I Cor. 7:10-11) Remarriage after a divorce that was not caused by fornication or the desertion of a lost spouse is adultery

(Matthew 19:9).

Secondly, remarriage is not permitted if the person you are marrying has been put away because they were the guilty party. Matthew 19:9 states,

And I say unto you, Whosoever shall put away his wife, except it be for fornication, and shall marry another, committeth adultery: and <u>whoso marrieth her which is put away doth commit adultery</u>.

If you marry someone who has been divorced because they cheated on their spouse then when you marry them you commit adultery. So remarriage to these people is forbidden.

Thirdly, remarriage is not permitted in the case where YOU are the guilty party in divorce. Notice in the same way you wouldn't be permitted to marry a person if they were guilty, the same would apply to you if you were guilty. This may seem harsh but the Bible must be our final authority. Consider Proverbs 6:32-33,

But <u>whoso committeth adultery</u> with a woman lacketh understanding: he that doeth it destroyeth his own soul. A wound and dishonor shall he get; and <u>his reproach shall not be wiped away.</u>

Once you commit adultery your reproach is not wiped away. Now please don't get me wrong. I am NOT saying that people in this situation that have gotten remarried should divorce their current spouse and stay single. I do not think that people should be kicked out of the church or barred from service. Nor do I believe that they are living in "perpetual adultery". As long as that person has gotten right with God and has sought forgiveness from the innocent party then who am I to judge. David committed adultery with Bathsheba and then murdered a man to cover it up. Yet David was one of the greatest kings to ever live (and he's coming back to reign as a king in the Millennial Kingdom) who wrote many scriptures that we all love dearly. Should we stop reading the Psalms because of what David did? No. But let's also not forget that whenever the life of David is brought up his sinful affair with Bathsheba is also brought up. Almost 3000 years later and David's reproach is still not wiped away.

Chapter 7
THE ESPOUSAL THEORY DEBUNKED

The Espousal Theory, as it has been called, is an anti-Biblical mess that was invented in the minds of the "once-married" Pharisees to get around what God has clearly said because it goes against their self-righteous traditions. This theory was popularized by Stinnett Ballew, a Baptist evangelist out of Resaca, GA, in his book, "The Home, America's Number One Problem". In his book he makes the claim that Matthew 19:9 and the "fornication clause" is referring to a case where a man finds out his espoused wife is not a virgin, so he puts her away, like the case of Mary and Joseph (Matthew 1:20-22). He thinks this fornication is referring to sex BEFORE marriage and not after. This comes from his misunderstanding of the word "fornication". In his book he says it is "sex before marriage" (pg. 27) and that it is not dealing with something that takes place "years after marriage" but with "someone who had just gotten married and found out his wife was not a virgin" (pg. 28). Mr. Ballew states in his book that Jesus was not giving a new stipulation to divorce in Matthew 19:9 but was giving "the grounds for which Moses permitted a man to put away his wife" (pg. 19). This is completely ludicrous when you simply read the verses. The Pharisees knew that in the Old Testament a man could put away his wife for "any uncleanness" (Deut. 24:1) that is why they ask him in Matthew 19:3 if it is "lawful for a man to put away his wife for every cause". This has nothing to do with the question of a man finding out his espoused wife is not a virgin. What to do in that situation was already established by Mosaic law in Deuteronomy 22:13-21,

> *13 If any man take a wife, and go in unto her, and hate her,*

> *14 And give occasions of speech against her, and bring up an evil name upon her, and say, <u>I took this woman, and when I came to her, I found her not a maid</u>:*

> *15 Then shall the father of the damsel, and her mother, take and bring forth the tokens of the damsel's virginity unto the elders of the city in the gate:*

> *16 And the damsel's father shall say unto the elders, I gave my daughter unto this man to wife, and he hateth her;*

> *17 And, lo, he hath given occasions of speech against her, saying, I found not thy daughter a maid; and yet these are the tokens of my daughter's virginity. And they shall spread the cloth before the elders of the city.*

> *18 And the elders of that city shall take that man and chastise him;*

> *19 And they shall amerce him in an hundred shekels of silver, and give them unto the father of the damsel, because he hath brought up an evil name upon a virgin of Israel: and she shall be his wife; he may not put her away all his days.*

> *20 <u>But if this thing be true, and the tokens of virginity be</u>*

not found for the damsel:

21 *Then they shall bring out the damsel to the door of her father's house, and <u>the men of her city shall stone her with stones that she die</u>: because she hath wrought folly in Israel, to play the whore in her father's house: so shalt thou put evil away from among you.*

If you read the verses you see that if a man proves his newly wedded wife is not a virgin then they take her out and stone her. There is no divorce, there is no putting away, there is no bill of divorcement, there is no going out to be another man's wife (Deut. 24:1-3). There is only stoning. This is reiterated more specifically concerning engaged couples, like Mary and Joseph in Deuteronomy 22:23-24

If a damsel that is <u>a virgin be betrothed unto an husband</u> (for example Mary), and a man find her in the city, <u>and lie with her</u>; Then ye shall bring them both out unto the gate of that city, and <u>ye shall stone them with stones that they die</u>; the damsel, because she cried not, being in the city; and the man, because he hath humbled his neighbour's wife: so thou shalt put away evil from among you.

To say that Jesus is somehow restating Jewish law and that he's referring to these passages can barely be called a "theory", its more like the mental gymnastics of preachers who try and act like the pope with the Bible!

Deuteronomy 22 is dealing with a woman who is found out not be a virgin. The terms "divorce/bill of divorcement" are not to be found in the passage. Let's look at Deuteronomy 24:1-4,

When a man hath taken a wife, and married her, and it come to pass that she find no favour in his eyes, because he hath found some uncleanness in her: then let him write her a <u>bill of divorcement</u>, and give it in her hand, and <u>send her out of his house</u>.

And when she is departed out of his house, <u>she may go and be another man's wife</u>.

And if the latter husband hate her, and write her a bill of divorcement, and giveth it in her hand, and sendeth her out of his house; or if the latter husband die, which took her to be his wife;

<u>Her former husband, which sent her away, may not take her again to be his wife, after that she is defiled</u>; for that is abomination before the Lord: and thou shalt not cause the land to sin, which the Lord thy God giveth thee for an inheritance.

This is referring to people who have been married and decide to get divorced. When this happens the husband writes the wife a bill of divorcement and she can go be another man's husband. She may not, however, return to her former husband.

These two passages are completely different and it's obvious which one Jesus and the Pharisees are discussing, the one with divorce and writing of bills, which would be Deuteronomy 24 NOT Deuteronomy 22. Unfortunately Mr. Ballew missed the mark on this one completely and added his own private interpretation of the scriptures. He even goes so far as to say that even if this situation happened (as he described) that it still does not permit remarriage (pg. 30). That's right, folks, according to Brother Ballew, if you find out on your wedding night that your wife is not a virgin after she told you that she was then you must either stay with her and live with it or divorce her and remain celibate for the rest of your life. This is the mode of operation though for most men who refuse to believe the scriptures when it comes to this subject.

Chapter 8
THE HUSBAND OF ONE WIFE

This debate intensifies even more once we get into the territory of a pastor. There are some preachers that are on the "once-married" side who are actually fairly gracious to divorced people and those going through one. This grace, though, finds it's hard end when a man who is divorced is a preacher or wants to be a preacher! The men who hold to this position are brutal in their attacks on a man who would even dare stay in the ministry after going through a divorce, especially when that man decides to remarry. Without bringing too much personal experiences into this, let me just say that I, Andrew Sluder, have only had one woman in my entire life. The woman I am married to right now is the only wife I have ever had. The first time I ever kissed her was on our wedding day. In no way at all could it EVER be said that I have "two living wives" YET I have had 4 preachers and one mission board that have gone so far as to call me and break fellowship with me simply because I have twice-married preachers behind my pulpit. When I've questioned them about the things I've wrote in previous chapters everyone of them (along with many others who I've had this conversation with) without exception always end the conversation with something along the lines of, "Well I see what you're saying but I still believe what I believe". Such biblical ignorance and puffed up arrogance is why Laodicea is in full swing. I had a preacher tell me (not hearsay, not rumors, his mouth to my ear) that he one time had a man preach for him and did not know that he was twice married until after the man preached. This guy takes his pulpit out in the parking lot, douses it in lighter fluid and TORCHES the thing! Talk about a nut case! I could go on and on but I digress. Lets now examine the most controversial verse in the Bible when it comes to this debate.

This is a true saying, If a man desire the office of a bishop, he desireth a good work. A bishop must then be blameless, <u>the husband of one wife</u>...

What many have interpreted this to mean is that if a man has been divorced and remarried then he is not the husband of one wife. He has had two wives, some would even say that he has "two-living wives", a phrase I heard all the time growing up. Now here is the question that must be asked at this point when dealing with men that think a divorced and remarried man cannot preach/pastor (there are a few men, very few, who think it's OK for the man to preach but not pastor). The question is this, "Do you believe that this verse is talking about one wife at a time or one and done?" All of them will respond, "One and done". I then ask them, "What about if my wife dies? Can I remarry then?" All them will answer, "Well, uh, yeah, of course if she dies you can remarry." This is where they officially paint themselves in a corner. I'll then say, "Okay, so you DON'T believe in 'one and done'. You believe in 'one at a time' but you make the only exception death." At this point they usually will accept this "sudden change" in terminology and agree. I then ask them, "So you if you accept the exception of death from Romans 7 then why don't you also accept the exceptions of fornication and abandonment?" This may shock you, but they never have a reply other than, "Well I just don't think a divorced man is qualified." So there you have it. It comes down to what they "think". This is no different than the contemporary crowd talking about "feelings". Remember this, folks, a legitimate divorce renders the marriage void. "She is not my wife and I am not her husband" (Hosea 2:2) "Her FORMER husband" (Deuteronomy 24:4) "Thou HAST HAD (past tense) five husbands" (John 4:18). This means that if you have a wife and you get divorced then you now have no wife. If you get remarried then you will have ONE wife. Only in the minds of the Pharisaical Baptist mini-popes does this math make sense....$(1-1)+1=2$. If you will accept the exception of death then you must accept the other two as well. This isn't a buffet, you either eat what is being served or you don't eat at all! Believe it or not I actually had a pastor in my area who had been listening to my videos online concerning this subject who recognized the logical fallacy of only accepting death as the exception. But instead of humbling himself, admitting he was wrong and taking a stand on biblical truth he decides to go the opposite direction and say that remarriage after death disqualifies you as well! Talk about the "fear of the brethren"! These guys would rather pervert the scriptures than have the "brethren" break fellowship with them!

What the conversation usually turns into is no longer a matter of the phrase "husband of one" but the phrases "blameless" and "one that ruleth his own house well". The problem that both of these "qualifications" pose is that first of all, no pastor is truly blameless in the sense of "sinless". Just because you may think that divorce is blameworthy enough to disqualify a man from the pulpit doesn't mean that everyone does. In fact, since I've made my position public some years ago I have found that the vast majority of people agree with me, including many who go to churches pastored by hard-line "once-married" guys. If you personally don't want to sit under a divorced man then that is YOUR business but just because you don't like it doesn't mean the man is disqualified.

Secondly, a man can be ruling his house to the best of his ability and STILL have marriage issues because his wife refuses to get right with God. I can't make my wife do anything. She has a freewill just like anyone else. We live in America, she is over 18. She doesn't have to do a thing I say according to the law of the land. If she wants to go out and leave that is HER business. I've seen men that were doing everything right, who loved their wives and who were not hypocrites at home that had their marriages fall apart because their wife gave into the flesh or simply didn't want to live the Christian life anymore. If my wife ever decides to leave then she will no longer be a part of "my house", she will have made her decision to go. Let us also not overlook the fact that contextually this phrase isn't even directly speaking of the wife but of the children! The rest of the phrase is "having his children in subjection with all gravity." When was the last time that you heard of preachers demanding that one of his buddies step down because he is dealing with a rebellious teenager? When is the last time a pastor was demanded to step down because he had children that were disobedient? See how this opens Pandora's Box?

The reason that they pitch a fit about this one, besides the fact that they are misinterpreting scripture, is because this is the only one they've never been guilty of! Going through this list would knock out most, if not all, of the pastors in America today. I know plenty of men that aren't "given to hospitality" or aren't "apt to teach". Could I demand they step down and then break fellowship with them? Do you see the pure HYPOCRISY of the "once-married" crowd? They pick and choose which qualifications they want to enforce and somehow this is the only one they seem to focus on. Madness!

We will end this chapter with a simple grammar lesson. Notice the Bible says "must BE" in I Timothy 3:2. The word "be" is present tense. That means that the bishop must be, at this PRESENT time, the husband of one wife. It does not say "must have had only one wife". This is a forbiddance of polygamy, more than one wife at time, NOT a forbiddance of having more than one wife in a lifetime. Remember that polygamy was never forbidden in the Old Testament. In fact, God didn't even show disapproval of it and went so far as to say that He gave David his enemies' wives (II Samuel 12:8). But with the coming in of a new dispensation and with Christ using marriage to symbolize his relationship with the church (Ephesians 5:25-33) we see a shift in the concept of marriage concerning polygamy. New Testament marriage is always seen as one man and one woman being faithful to each other. The qualification is given here because at the time the culture would still have cases of polygamy occurring. This verse shows us the transition of what New Testament marriage should be.

Chapter 9
THE "HISTORIC POSITION"

I was once told by a man who held the "once-married" position that no one use to believe in "twice-married" preachers before the 50's and 60's. He said that it was just "understood" that divorced and remarried people were committing adultery and were no longer eligible for the ministry. I will now show you through documented historical evidence that that statement is complete bologna. In quoting these men, it does NOT mean that I endorse them, all of their doctrinal views or the denominations they were apart of.

"By parity of reason, it is adultery for any man to marry again, so long as he has a wife alive, yea, although they were divorced; unless that divorce had been for the cause of adultery: In that only case there is no scripture which forbids to marry again" (John Wesley, Sermon on the Mount, Discourse 3)

"V. Adultery or fornication committed after a contract, being detected before marriage, giveth just occasion to the innocent party to dissolve that contract. In the case of adultery after marriage, it is lawful for the innocent party to sue out a divorce: and, after the divorce, to marry another, as if the offending party were dead.

VI. Although the corruption of man be such as is apt to study arguments unduly to put asunder those whom God hath joined together in marriage: yet nothing but adultery, or such willful desertion as can no way be remedied by the Church or civil magistrate, is cause sufficient of dissolving the bond of marriage." (Westminster Confession of Faith, Chapter 14, Articles 5 & 6, 1647)

"Only one exception does Christ give to the rule, Matthew 5:32...Fornication means unfaithfulness of one spouse to the other in the marriage relation. Illicit intercourse with another is given as a just cause for severance of the marriage tie...Since the guilty party in such a case has already broken the marital bond, the innocent party does not on his or her part break it in obtaining a divorce... (Our Daily Bread Home Devotions, F.E. Pasche, Lutheran Minister, 1929)

"Instead of its being lawful for a man to put away his wife for every cause, he acknowledged only one justifiable cause, infidelity to the marriage vow. The husband alone had title to the body of the wife and the wife alone to the body of the husband. An offense against this authority justified absolute divorce, for thereby was the unity of one flesh broken...Divorce on the ground of adultery leaves the innocent party free to marry." (The Four Gospels, B.H. Carroll, late President of Southwestern Baptist Theological Seminary, 1916)

The following excerpts are from "Dr. Rice, Here is my Question" (John R. Rice, Founder of the Sword of the Lord, 1962)

"As I understand the scriptures, according to Matthew 5:31-32 and Matthew 19:9, fornication, that is, a course of continued adultery, <u>brings the possibility of divorce</u>...This is the one exception which Jesus Himself makes."

"Sometimes restoration of a marriage is impossible, and in such case <u>divorce is permitted, although it is not commanded</u>. As I understand the scriptures also, <u>divorce means the right to remarry</u>."

"<u>In that passage (Romans 7:1-3) the scripture does not indicate that a woman who has divorced her husband and marries another has two husbands. That is modern talk, not Bible language</u>."
"If his former companion has married again, it would mean that her lying with another man has broken the marriage and would <u>give him a right to be married again</u>."

"<u>I think it is clear from the Bible that one who has a right to divorce has a right to remarry</u>."

"I do not believe in passing a rule that one who has ever been divorced cannot be a deacon or preacher. <u>And my reason is very simple; there is no such rule in the Bible</u>."

(Moving on from Rice)

"If one violates the tie by unchaste behavior, that is, by illicit relations with a third party, <u>the innocent one is free</u>

to divorce the unfaithful one and to marry someone else." (H.A. Ironside, Commentary on Matthew)

"The Lord thus graciously provided a way of escape for the innocent party. He or she is allowed an unencumbered divorce and is free to remarry, in contrast to one who seeks to end a marriage on other and frivolous grounds. Adultery breaks the marriage bond and the consequent divorce sets the injured partner free to marry again. No one has any right to cast stones at such an individual or to treat the innocent party as though he or she were the guilty party." (John Phillips, Commentary on Matthew)

"Particularly objectionable, is the legalist's claim that a remarriage following a scriptural divorce involves ' two living husbands' (or wives, as the case may be). This claim, is tantamount to accusing the remarried person of being either a bigamist or a polygamist. Such an accusation is both untrue and libelous." (John Phillips, Commentary on I Timothy 3:2)

This is just a small number of references from throughout the years that CLEARLY show that the matter of divorce and remarriage has NOT been viewed like the modern day Baptist Pharisees view it. This wasn't invented in the 50's and 60's by men trying to justify themselves. It's a biblical truth that has been clearly seen since the writings of the "originals".

Chapter 10
THE HISTORIC CATHOLIC POSTION

The Roman Catholic Church is no doubt the Great Whore of Revelation 17. Down through the years she has developed many strange and heretical views. Some of them concerning marriage. In this chapter I will show you exactly where the modern day idea of the "once-married" crowd comes from. It is none other than the Roman Catholic Church. Below I will give you historical references from Catholic Catechisms, popes, priests and scholars.

"Between the baptized, a ratified and consummated marriage cannot be dissolved by any human power or for any reason other than death." (Catholic Catechism, Article 6)

"A faithful woman who has left an adulterous husband and is marrying another who is faithful, let her be prohibited from marrying; if she has married, let her not receive communion until the man she has left shall have departed this life, unless illness should make this an imperative necessity." (Synod of Elvira, 300 AD)

Synod of Arles (314 AD) counsels young men that had dismissed their wives for adultery "should take no second wife".

"In respect to all cases the rule is kept that whoever marries another man, while her husband is still alive, must be held an adulteress, and must be granted no leave to do penance unless one of the men shall have died." (Pope Innocent I, 401-417AD)

"V. If anyone shall say that the bond of matrimony can be dissolved for the cause of heresy, or of injury due to cohabitation, or of willful desertion; let him be anathema.

VII. If anyone shall say that the Church has erred in having taught, and in teaching that, according to the teaching of the Gospel and the Apostles, the bond of matrimony cannot be dissolved, and that neither party, not even the innocent, who has given no cause by adultery, can contract another marriage while the other lives, and that he, or she, commits adultery who puts away an adulterous wife, or husband, and marries another; let him be anathema." (Council of Trent, Canon 5 & 7, 24th Session)

A brief study of history will show that the one the main reasons for the Protestant Reformation flourishing in England was because King Henry VIII wanted a divorce from his wife, Catherine. But Pope Clement VII wouldn't give him one. So he broke away from the Catholic church and started the Church of England. The Catholic church has always held the anti-biblical view that marriage can only end until a spouse dies without exception. The Catholic church puts unbiblical requirements concerning marriage on it's priests as well, forbidding them to even get married. Paul warned about this end times prohibition on marriage in I Timothy 4:1,

Now the Spirit speaketh expressly, that in the latter times some shall depart from the faith, giving heed to seducing spirits and doctrines of devils; Speaking lies in hypocrisy; having their conscience seared with a hot iron; <u>Forbidding to marry</u>, and commanding to abstain from meats..."

The Bible says that anyone who forbids marriage is "giving heed to seducing spirits and doctrines of devils". "Seducing" comes from the same word we get seduction from, which is used primarily in connection to sexual sin. Like it or lump
when we begin to tell people that they cannot marry we will by default open the door for more sexual sin in the life of a Christian. Paul clearly says in I Corinthians 7:1-2 that the way to avoid fornication is to MARRY! If you cannot contain, then marry. It's better to marry than to burn according to Paul in I Corinthians 7:9. The Catholic church forbids their priests from getting married and also forbids any of their members from remarrying after a divorce. The modern day Baptist's have unfortunately found themselves agreeing with half of the Roman Catholic position on marriage.

Chapter 11
THE LAST STRAW

The reason I decided to write this small book is because I simply am fed up with the constant berating and attacking of men who have had to go through a divorce yet still decided to stay in the ministry. The attacks I get for simply believing this and using guys who are divorced are vicious enough. I couldn't even begin to imagine the things that a man who is actually divorced must face from the "brethren". Friends of mine who have been through a divorce have been straight up lied on, talked about, been called adulterers and their wives called "whores". I think it's time to put up or shut up. Refute what's been written or take a seat and mind your business.

I think it is very interesting that right in the middle of the greatest chapter on divorce and remarriage in the Pauline Epistles (I Corinthians 7) that Paul makes this statement (vs. 20),

Let every man abide in the same calling where in he was called.

That doesn't sound like Paul was encouraging or demanding anybody to get out of the ministry. Now don't get me wrong, I'm not defending "skirt chasers" or people who have flippantly left their spouse because they couldn't get along. But I am defending those people who, by no fault of their own, have suffered this awful thing called divorce. I have never been through one and hope I never do. But I have friends and family who have been through them and let me say this, those people are some of the godliest people I know. Some of the best preachers I have ever had the privilege to hear have been divorced. Some of the best Bible students on planet earth are people who have been divorced. I am of the strong belief that God can use anybody, anywhere and at anytime and He doesn't need anybody's permission to do it either. I am not in the ministry of putting other men out of the ministry. There may be some men who have had questionable marriage situations that I may not agree with. I have downright refused to preach for some guys because of this but at the same time I'm not interested in trying to get them thrown out of their pulpits. At the end of the day every man must be persuaded in his own mind. If you don't want to be associated with divorced preachers then that is your business. You have that right. But you cannot say that it is Bible, you cannot legitimately say he's disqualified and you sure can't change what the Scriptures say.

If you are a divorced person in the church I want you to know that I am not against you. I do not think you are a second class Christian. I do not think you should be hindered from serving because of your marital status. If you are a preacher who has been divorced I encourage you to stay in the ministry. Keep pastoring, keep preaching, keep being an evangelist. Will it be hard? Yes. But will it be worth it? YES! If you are a preacher who has gotten out of the ministry because of divorce I encourage you to pick up your sword once more and get back in the fight. I'm sorry if you have been berated and ostracized from the ministry because you went through a divorce (if you were the innocent party). I'm sorry that men who should know better have forced their anti-biblical view on you. But know this, there is a preacher in Asheville, NC who is FOR you! I am in your corner and am praying that God uses you more than he ever has! No doubt I will get labeled for this even more than I have already because now it is officially in writing. That's fine. I'm more interested in what the Book says than their opinions anyway. This book will stand the attacks because of one simple thing...it is the TRUTH! Not because I said it but because God said it! Say what you will, rant and rave all you want but according to the authority of God's Holy Word you can be "DIVORCED BUT <u>NOT</u> DEMOTED"!!!

Made in the USA
Monee, IL
16 February 2022